# GOD DON'T WANT TO WANT TO BEAT YOU HE WANT TO BLESS YOU!!!

QUEEN VANESSA BANKS

# GOD DON'T WANT TO BEAT YOU HE WANT TO BLESS YOU!!!

Scripture quotations are taken from Holy Bible., Today's New International
Version TNIV. International Bible Society, Colorado Springs, CO., 2001,2006.
Used by permission of Zondervan. All rights reserved worldwide.

iUniverse books may be ordered through booksellers or by contacting:

iUniverse
1663 Liberty Drive
Bloomington, IN 47403
www.iuniverse.com
844-349-9409

Because of the dynamic nature of the Internet, any web addresses or
links contained in this book may have changed since publication and may
no longer be valid. The views expressed in this work are solely those
of the author and do not necessarily reflect the views of the publisher,
and the publisher hereby disclaims any responsibility for them.

Any people depicted in stock imagery provided by Getty Images are
models, and such images are being used for illustrative purposes only.
Certain stock imagery © Getty Images.

ISBN: 978-1-6632-3953-2 (sc)
ISBN: 978-1-6632-3954-9 (e)

Print information available on the last page.

iUniverse rev. date: 05/06/2022

*Photo by Queen Vanessa*

# WHEN I THINK OF MY LIFE, I THINK OF THE WONDERFUL WORKS OF GOD HANDS.

God don't want to beat us He want to bless us
was created to help you understand, the ways
of this world has nothing to do with you.

Sometimes we beat ourselves up. That's
a weapon satan use against you.

He will kill steal and destroy you or all
your works, our children, families and
communities. We must STOP, beating
ourselves and loving ourselves and trust

God loves you more just as much as He
loves our ancestors and If you only believe
in His works. I am a living witness.

If we just stop and join forces with who can
move mountains and cease the winds to

commanding the waves of the ocean. Can you do that? Do you know anybody that can?

I do we call him Jesus, trust in Him for He'll be your personal Lord and Savior,

GOD got us Do we got Him? Trust me He doesn't want to beat us. He really wants to bless us. But we must listen to Him. Be blessed… Queen Vanessa

# Foreword

I first heard of *God Don't Want to Beat You He Want to Bless You* while on a call with Queen Vanessa. She asked, "Melody, you used to be a teacher, can you take a look at my book and fix any mistakes? Like grammar and punctuation and things? I know I did stuff wrong like start sentences with the word 'and' and I know you aren't supposed to do that."

I agreed but first asked more about the book and its purpose. After hearing about the idea, I asked her if she wanted it to sound formal or if she wanted to sound casual, like in a conversation. "And honestly we don't talk the way we write because when we talk we don't really use complete sentences for instance I just started this sentence with the word 'and' because we often do start sentences that way when we talk and when we talk we just go on and on and if we were to write out exactly how we talk it would often be just one long, run-on sentence without the correct punctuation and pauses and things that we add to written work."

We ultimately decided that this piece of work would benefit from being written in the same way that Queen Vanessa speaks. I can hear her words on the page. It is her voice that shines through and, as a journal, it does not conform to the same expectations of writing that we expect from novels or essays.

I am thankful to Queen Vanessa for sharing her thoughts, perspectives, and experiences. I am thankful to Queen Vanessa for sharing prompts that encourage me to explore my own thoughts and fears. I am thankful to Queen Vanessa for all of the work she has done in the community and for the community.

And to you, dear reader, enjoy this journey into Queen Vanessa's world and allow her guidance to bring you to a place of love, acceptance, and power. Don't let your fear keep you from knowing and loving yourself, from knowing and loving a Higher Power. Embrace it.

Melody B. Hernandez
San Francisco, 2022

# Table of Contents

## God Don't Want to Beat Us
## He Want to Bless Us

**Dedicated to**
All God children who battle with mental
incapability of is God real?
Yes, He's as real as you and I.

Dear God, I love you so much,
thank you now and forever

"I would like to thank God for
considering me" (Queen Vanessa)
Jeremiah 1

Thank you, God, for my beloved parents:
Robert Earl Banks Sergeant of Korean War
Sept 25th, 1931- May 14th, 1992

Mother of many generations Alice Marie Blunt Banks
Oct 9th, 1930- July 21, 2014

Served her life as a spiritual warrior-
caregiver & community activist devoted wife,
mother, grand & great/grandmother

To my children I love you three so much I thank God
for giving me
King Dishon
Queen Antionay
Queen Alayia

To my grandsons King Destin & Reynardo. Queen Grandma love you so much, King Grandsons always follow the leader which is God.

Queen Grandma want you to lead this world not follow it. God bless you no matter what happens King Grandsons &, and my unborn grandchildren I will always be with you, always trust God, for Jesus to have your back and front. To all the readers you are loved, and you are needed. No matter where you are at in life. Your works will not be void. I love you and so does Jesus Trust me God want to bless us He has plenty!

*Photo by Queen Vanessa*

**You Are Not Alone!**
**When you are feeling sad, abandoned, hurt,**
**mistreated, manipulated, fearful, unsure,**
**unworthy, low self- esteem, when there's**
**negativity all round you in your home,**
**your schools, and your community.**

**Stay focus there are still good**
**positive peoples and outcomes**
**You Are Not Alone when the world feels**
**like it's on your shoulders, your stressed**
**out don't feel like God isn't nearby.**

**Look up stare into the clouds,**
**You Are Not Alone.**

**God is with you *clouds are the
dust of His footprints*
You Are Never Alone!**

**Nuham 1:3** The Lord is slow to anger and great in power, and the Lord will by no means leave the guilty unpunished, In the whirlwind and storm in His way and clouds are the dust beneath His feet.

# YOU MATTER NOW AND FOREVER
*"If I tell you once I can tell you twice you matter"- queen vanessa*

This message is dedicated to everyone who's born into the world. Be mindful you weren't born into poverty; poverty was born unto you
I pray that I can speak into your life- bring you hope you will never forget.

I pray every word I say comes for the most High, Holy Spirit, and my brother Jesus Christ.

I hope to make you laugh, share a few tears and think I 'am praying by the end of my message you'll know exactly how precious you're to heaven and earth!

As a culture of people residing here in America as children of God. We all have been striped, misled, and for so long unfocused on who we really are!
Born queens and kings. As people if we don't know our past, understand our present. Confused at awe we will have a bigger problem trying to make it in the future without God.

So, here's a wise old saying if you don't know your past, not up with your current affairs your presence, you're bound to have an off balanced future.

Mother's Day weekend May 11, 2012, I am Every Women: Mobilizing and Empowering Mothers, Sisters,

Daughters and Aunts to Lead the Way to Better Health hosted by the Black Coalition Aids/ Rafiki Wellness.
A group of Mothers was taught by the great Dr. Brenda Wade, author of
*What Mama Couldn't Tell Us About Love, Emotional Legacy of Racism by Celebrating Our Light.* A must read to understand how African Americans terms and conditions in the era of slavery.

# YOU MATTER NOW AND FOREVER
*"If I tell you once I can tell you twice you matter"- queen vanessa*

Taught us to express these simple words into our life:

- I'm worthily
- I am deserving
- I love me unconditional- (created you own beat and tune, and plant good seeds into your life)

Often with all the things going on in the world, we don't find time to be still, enough to even trust God.

We all have to learn my sisters and brothers if God wanted life to be everyday all days to be good. We would be strong, and He'll be weak.

Young people trust me. We are nothing. I mean nothing young or old rich or poor blind or deaf. We're nothing without God

I speak to you by experiences **God don't Want to Beat Us. He Wants to Bless Us.**

I know the world painting you a picture that God not real. I know with all the murders, killings and disaster in the world, it seems unreal there's no hope. Yes, it can and will be for you if you believe, God and his son Jesus Christ love you.

God wants to bless us read Psalms 100

*Shout for joy to the Lord all the earth*
*Worship the Lord with gladness come*
*before him with joyful songs*

*Know that the Lord is God*
*It is He who made us, and we are His*
*We are His people the sheep of His pasture*

*Enter his gates with thanksgiving*
*Scream to the courts with praise give*
*praise to Him and praise His name.*
*For the Lord is good and His love endures*
*forever His faithfulness continues through*
*all generations.*

*We all need to remember from one*
*generation to the next God Don't Want to*
*Beat Us. He Wants to Bless Us…*

# WE'RE ALL IN THIS TOGETHER:
*"Keep yourself from fallen apart" -queen vanessa*

Everywhere I go I hear people say young people today don't have no respect.

It's a lot of grown folks also who don't have no respect for themselves or others.
Respect isn't giving by age categories it's a normal to give to everyone.

I recommend that respect shall be carried with you like an ID, grab it before you leave your home like a jacket, your house and car keys.

Respect yourself first, self- care tell yourself 'hello' and 'good morning', tell yourself together we can make it. Speak into your life!

Smile at yourself, respect your items, your time & conditions, your space, be thankful for the Muni driver who delivered you to your destination safely. Be thankful when you leave home safe and return safe with your family and love ones.

Respecting those simple things simply builds that ounces of love that weighs a lot in all our lives

If you learn to respect yourself ii is easier to respect others be the trend setter. (BREAK THE CYCLE)

## WE'RE ALL IN THIS TOGETHER:
*"Keep yourself from fallen apart" -queen vanessa*

Example:

This young lady, I grew up with as a childhood community member we survived our teenage years in the streets of San Francisco.

As adults I tried to help her out with a few dollars. She was a drug addict. One day I couldn't help her, I told her No twice.
Then turned around and gave her a dollar.
I really didn't have myself.

After she received my dollar, she immediately cursed me, called me names, if thou I was entitled to give to her. I don't mind giving.

I have learned now to be careful who I give too, unappreciative people, ungrateful, rude lack of manners, is a sign of NO Respect....

Instead of reacting with a reaction in a negative manner, I walked away.
I was upset with her yes, but that was her flesh attacking the both of us.

She apologized asked for forgiveness, I accepted her forgiveness. Now that's respect and love.

Here's the keys to life, God's going to judge us on what we do to help one another.

## WE'RE ALL IN THIS TOGETHER:
*"Keep yourself from fallen apart" -queen vanessa*

We're all in this together. The have and have nots, God going to judge us according to our works and obedience's. If we learn to treat each other with respect it goes a long way.

Don't worry about the next person lack thereof be a trendsetter. Why follow when you can lead? (BREAK THE CYCLE)

Believe, **God Don't Want to Beat Us. He Want to Bless Us**!

Be Blessed....

## ALL WE NEED IS TO GET OUR MINDS RIGHT ON WHAT MATTERS.

*"Live life and count it all joy the bad, good, pretty and ugly"* -queen vanessa

Of course, there are things we all need to slow down and rethink about. Nine times out of ten even stop doing.

We can put more hurt, pain and confusion in our own lives most of the times.

First signs which are a big no: doubt, fear, worrying, or the lack of self-control)

Another thing that messes with us achieving as a culture of people.

HATING

Hating endures from a lack of:
Understanding
Love from others often causes us to be bitter
Self-love if you don't love yourself. How can you love someone
else? (Think about it)
Food
Money
Housing
Confidence
Self- esteem

Hating is the biggest sign of not known who you are.

I didn't say what you have. What you know is more important.

Take time in your life to read your history, understand why the world has its life issues, has nothing to do with you per say, but your presents play a major part on the world going around.

## WE'RE ALL IN THIS TOGETHER:
*"Keep yourself from fallen apart" -queen vanessa*

I know it's hard to love others at times. Listen to me it is harder to hate. Trust me. It takes to much energy and besides. We have others doing that for us. You're born into God hands & plans it's our job to stay covered by His blood.

Why continue to do it to others? Unless you are a hater like them?

Listen I want to really share this, it's important I to have longevity in your spiritual tool kit!

It takes a greater number of facial muscles to frown than it does to smile.

It takes 37 muscles to frown and 22 muscle to smile.

So, **SMILE**

## According to snopes.com Muscles to smile and frown:
"Yet smiling is not just good for the community in which the sad sack or grouch lives. It is also beneficial to the person doing the grinning.

Facial expressions do not merely signal what one feels but actually contribute to the feeling If we smile when we don't feel like it our mood will elevate despite ourselves. Likewise, faking frowns bring on a sense of much like the world that day!"

# WE'RE ALL IN THIS TOGETHER:
*"Keep from fallen apart"- queen vanessa*

When you have a friend like Jesus. You have a reason to smile, He will never let you down like people. I'm sure you heard the old saying

He might not be there when you want Him, but He always on time.
If you believe He will never forsake you, see my God is Awesome!

He taught me how to like and dislike but never to use more of my energy with dislikes.

No, I don't like the fact people racist against others because the color of one's skin.

Reasons to smile. I'm glad I learned Scope theory.

Exactly why we shall smile a lot!

It's not our fault God created us all, but it's our fight, the battle is won by His stripes. By nature, we are all born sinners, but we can heal from our sins.
So, trust me when I say **God Don't Want to Beat Us, He wants to Bless Us!**

Be blessed

# Choices

*"Make choices in your life you will never have to regret"* -queen vanessa

It is true, we all hurt in ways that we don't understand at times.

Trust God He know what He's doing for your life.

Not all mishaps be our final destination.

There's a saying, if we know better, we will do better we all have **Choices.**
There are a few words we need to be thankful for.
Embed them in our heart like a favorite song.

Lord help me to make wiser better choices for my life.

Lord helps me to communicate with kindness and understanding.

Lord teach me to prepare a table with you.

What He means by "preparing a table for two". It's simple spending time with Jesus. Try this, close your door and focus on caring loving sprits. Just be still, quiet and listen. Close your eyes and be thankful and be patience, He knows what your needs are. He wants to provide for you! Life with ups and down for you can lean on Him.

Not only when in need or in trouble.

Lord can you teach me how to need you, for everything in my life, teach me.

Lord knows all generations endure Peer Pressure Example:

At times you may feel you have to choose between a family member and your pressure?

What if you wanted to stay out on a Saturday night with your friends?

# Choices
*"Make choices in your life you will never
have to regret" -queen vanessa*

I know but, in your heart, you really want to go home.
Catch up on some schoolwork study or get ready for
church.

Instead, you go out and convince yourself you won't
party too hard, and you will be able to get up the next
morning.

Understand early in life school not going to teach you
everything you will need to nag aviate in life. Peer
pressure is a world element- everyone experiences,
but we have Choices.

It is okay to be alone, spending time with yourself
taking time to dream and map out your future.

It okay to be a loner, and do me a big favorite listen
to my voice,

You are never a loner; God's with you when you not
with yourself.
Whenever you feel doubtful, worried, depressed, or
fearful do not be.

God's trying to tell you now if you listening to me.

## God Don't Want to Beat Us.
## He Wants to Bless Us!

God loves you; you mean so much to Him.
God loves you more than anybody you can call, even Facebook or IG can't love you like Jesus.

Yes, more than our parents, brothers, sisters existing family and friends.
God is never double minded, He solid, He confident in His words and works
God not two faced. He is not going to judge you wrong; He will help you end your mistakes.

People will let you down no doubt satan will use people to distract you from your purpose. If you read the Bible for yourself an let the words mediate in your heart. He states it very clear in His words you will be the "head and not the tail".

# Choices
*"Make choices in your life you will never have to regret"-queen vanessa*

What's important to God, is us joining in His realm of understanding and love.

Know it may be hard to start loving somebody that hurt us. I whole heartly understand,

We can forgive and be forgiving.

I attended a conference in 2011, taught by Pastor Debra Simmons South Sacramento Christian Center.

If there are somethings that bothers you, or someone you dislike.

> (1).Write their name down on a piece of paper. (2). State how you forgive them and yourself. (3). Write in on tissue to flush or paper to burn.

Name the people places and things you want to forgiveness.
Flush/Burn Let it go it over with that how you learn the power of forgiveness.
We first need to learn how to use the tools, and don't be afraid to let go.

Trust me **God Don't Want to Beat Us. He Wants to Bless Us**.

**Choices** how sweet **choices** sound,

This one word I want each and every one of you to master is choices.

I am telling you master **choices,** and you can make wise ones for your life. If you pay attention- to yourself your surroundings and company, you keep.

Don't do drugs they been done for you already. The problem will still be there. We have been told.

# Choices

*"Make choices in your life you will never have to regret". -queen vanessa*

Don't use or sell drugs or sex workers madness. Study, read, stay in school, information changes every three years.
Educate yourself all your life for the rest of your life!

Don't waste time, if you think time moving slow, it's not time it's you.
Time is moving more rapidly than ever before the future is here.
As we get deeper into the future, time going to move even faster.

God said it will come a time.
When men will not know the night from day and day from night
**Choices** will save your life, God going to judge us all according to how we treat others.

Don't worry about the next individual(s) you are only accountable for your action.
In other words, no friends or family members going to be punished for your sins.

You have a **choice** in giving and receiving, be sure to give in love and receive in love as well

Keep in mind not everybody going to like nor love you for acknowledging or rocking with Jesus.

Remember you have a **choice** to think for your eternal life, do not be fooled by the ways of the world.

The devil made a **choice** to do wrong and go against God. Don't be foolish, make wiser **choices** off top don't go against God.

# Choices
*Make choices in your life you will never
have to regret-queen vanessa*

But remember we all have **choices** satan only mission is to kill, steal, and destroy not just your moments also your days and your life.
So, chose wisely and praise God. He's in the midst of it all!

He knows what you are going through- be careful what you say out loud. The devil has ears also.
If you just allow God/Jesus to use my testimonies to convince you my Sisters and Brothers. Be worthy of His love.

If you just trust in Him. He keeps His promise, all your storms will come to past.
He designed you into His image to be blessed not beat you down with hopeless.

Trust and do understand life lessons aren't always easy. They can be rewarding! And life changing, once you allow God to lead.

The Bible defines Basic Instruction Before Leaving Earth.
Which reflex back to **Choices**?
Always try to do a good deed and help others when you can.

If it's only a smile or a simple hello you can really makes a person day!
Do not block your life blesses, remember **choices** serve a better purpose than forces.

Remember violence don't hurt people, people hurt people make a **choice** be a trendsetter, the world needs and counting on you to make it a beautiful place.
Live Learn Teach
Be blessed

# Why Black Lives Matter:
*"God created all lives to matter: Black lives more essential to our cause." -queen vanessa*

In conclusion

I wanted to conclude with what has impacted African Americans even today in our era, we still fighting for our civic rights- urban social justice Black Lives Matter!

It's really discomforting and disturbing to learn right here in America, Fifty years later. All Martin Luther King Jr., fought to change, hasn't especially with attacks: War on Drugs, COVID-19 and poor peoples.

Black males and women are still being lynched and shot down in 2021.
I would say like animals, not even animals need to be murdered, under no circumstances.

Think about all the animals' rights advocates? None of them yet to intertwine into law, dogs shall not be trained to bite peoples as a weapon.

We must continue. The Struggle is Real- we must never forget our role in society.
Ask yourself how much do my Black life matter?

We the only race that's treated like crap. And it has been for centuries, we still struggle different from another races

To make matters worse we treat each other worse than other ethnic groups.

Does the world appreciate Black Life?
Blacks are the biggest settle for less, sellouts, we sellout to money, drugs, poor living conditions. You continue the list:
How much do Black Lives matter? Be Sold Out for God!

## Why Black Lives Matter:
*"God created all lives to matter: Black lives more essential to our cause." -queen vanessa*

Young people I say to you.

You have the chance to change the game, for your survival.

Understand how programs are written in operation to serve you.

Get involve with government read their blogs, newsletters, social media platforms and attend community meetings, live and virtual.

Learn to research and keep up with your current affairs Speak up and out for yourself and your children.

Do you best in school never give up. Never stop learning information change every three years. Lose your pride it's not your friend

Trust God.

I'm not against the Black Lives Matter movement

I have my own opinions- the focus shall be Black survival period, in America.

A child of God and an activist.
I'm able to see clear through His eyes

We got some folks pushing the Black Lives Matter as a political agenda

If we matter readers
What will you do to prove all lives matter?

# Why Black Lives Matter:

*"God created all lives to matter: Black lives more essential to our cause." -queen vanessa*

A Message from Queen Vanessa
Black Lives Matter because Jesus is Black

We are the first origins people on the planet
Evildoers have stripped us of our identity.
Of course, Black Lives Matter, ask Black people this?

How would the world exist without us?
There are no answers for that question, my friends we are the chosen people!

That's why we struggle different from the rest- be proud!
No need to second guess yourself.

Why Black Lives Matter?

God created you before your parents hooked up. He already considered your life with purpose. Why you matter!

Love you & God Bless you!
Queen Vanessa

*Photo by Queen Vanessa*

Sometimes you have to be careful what you ask God. You just might get it, then you might not. Remember God listening, so is satan, only satan mission is different (it) spirit hate you (it) comes to steal, kill and destroy everything about you.

Understand (it's) well equipped with your life plan:
You need to master in only God will for your life.
Because He knows they ways you shall go to
be greater, and remember you are purpose!
God Don't Want to Beat You He
Want to Bless You and Your Children.

*Photo by Queen Vanessa*

It's okay whenever you need to re-set your
life. Just never give up. Enjoy nature
**5 STEPS** to help you Re-set

1. Take a walk by the ocean
2. Sit next to a nice big tree or
flowers in your local parks.
3. Watch the clouds as they stroll
by daily, to make you smile.
4. Dance & Laugh out Loud
5. Think and Pray Always

With the presents of God blessings, Sun
shining waves roaring, trees change with
the seasons- leaves blowing clouds flowing
remember they're following you,
Clouds are the footprints of God.
God Don't Want to Beat You He Want to Bless You

## The City & County of San Francisco, CA
## Sutro Tower

*Photo by Queen Vanessa*

## No one going to love you like Jesus
## Believe that!

*"Believe"- queen vanessa*

What to Get to Know Me: Thank you- I want to know you too!

Hi, stay safe and blessed, and keep it classy and be a spiritual gangster.

Queen Vanessa's born and raised native Bayview Hunters Point, San Francisco CA. God Don't Want to Beat Us He Wants to Bless Us, is a motional testimony to help every generation, who might not experience church, or spirituality, inside their households. From my knowledge, African Americans membership and committeemen to the kingdom has declined since the crack epidemic. Spiritual is the most important element for the livelihood of Black/ African Americans, God allowed Queen Vanessa, to bring an authentic unique urban spiritual movement into reality. God not only in the church. I'm not currently a member of any church, but I was raised up in one. My mother was a natural born "spiritual warrior" But I'm an observer, listener and student of God, and His son Jesus. Who lead and guided my life this far? Whereas I'm looking forward to God using me, it will be my honor to serve with Him and for Him.

I know God trust me I'm very spiritual, and I know what God has for me, He has for you. First, we have to believe He will do any and everything your life desires: *God Don't Want to Beat Us He Wants to Bless Us.* Believe!

Queen Vanessa currently, resides in the Bay Area with her families. Queen Vanessa 's one of Born And Raised Survivors Community Developers upcoming urban social justice movements, member. She's an urban: grassroots organizer, film producer, author, motivational speaker, storyteller & spiritual advisor.

Queen Vanessa your life coach urban spiritual advisor here for you,
Email: yesvbanks@gmail.com
Like our Facebook page: Born and Raised Survivors
Journaling is the best self -help care you can give yourself and others. So often with technology, we're custom to forgive the pleasure of treasuring our thoughts and writing them down or simply sharing them with others.
Journaling is the best tool for self- preservation understanding your own emotional intelligences. The best part about herpetic journaling it's best to conduct with all your emotions elements: happy sad, fear, confused.

As a certified spiritual advisor challenging you to journal and open up your horizons. Trust God for everything! Queen Vanessa!

*Photo by Queen Vanessa*

"An important message: Don't let anyone capture you with empty philosophies and high-sounding nonsense that come from human thinking and from the spiritual power of this world, rather than from Christ" ....

The Word for You Today
December- January 2022
New Covenant Church Fellowship.,
2021 Celebration Inc.

**Sometimes silence is good sometime silence it's not good.**

**Journal a time you wished you spoke out.**

_____

_____

_____

_____

_____

_____

_____

_____

_____

_____

_____

_____

_____

_____

_____

_____

_____

_____

_____

_____

_____

_____

_____

_____

**Use your voice to heal others! People are in your life for a season and a reason enjoy them both. (Journal moments of comforting and discomforted situations.)**

_____

_____

_____

_____

_____

_____

_____

_____

_____

_____

_____

_____

_____

_____

_____

_____

_____

_____

_____

_____

_____

_____

---

---

---

---

---

---

---

---

---

---

---

---

---

---

---

---

---

---

---

---

---

---

---

---

---

---

**Reading and Writing is Healing Power!**

**Don't Be Afraid to Crossover (Die) It's okay to crossover: If you miss someone, journal to your loved ones.**

_____

_____

_____

_____

_____

_____

_____

_____

_____

_____

_____

_____

_____

_____

_____

_____

_____

_____

_____

_____

_____

_____

_____

**One day at a time be easy on yourself!**

# What do you like most about yourself?

_____

_____

_____

_____

_____

_____

_____

_____

_____

_____

_____

_____

_____

_____

_____

_____

_____

_____

_____

_____

_____

_____

_____

_____

_____

_____

_____

_____

_____

_____

_____

_____

_____

_____

_____

_____

_____

_____

_____

_____

_____

_____

_____

_____

_____

_____

_____

_____

_____

**Remember God loves you just the way you are….**

# Do you smile often or frown more (Be Honest)!

_____

_____

_____

_____

_____

_____

_____

_____

_____

_____

_____

_____

_____

_____

_____

_____

_____

_____

_____

_____

_____

_____

_____

_____

_____

_____

_____

_____

_____

_____

_____

_____

_____

_____

_____

_____

_____

_____

_____

_____

_____

_____

_____

_____

_____

_____

_____

_____

**God rather see you smiling and laughing it's good for your health.**

**Do you attend church service live or online? Who do you follow, and what you like about their spiritual messages?**

_____
_____
_____
_____
_____
_____
_____
_____
_____
_____
_____
_____
_____
_____
_____
_____
_____
_____
_____
_____
_____
_____
_____
_____
_____
_____

_____

_____

_____

_____

_____

_____

_____

_____

_____

_____

_____

_____

_____

_____

_____

_____

_____

_____

_____

_____

_____

_____

_____

_____

_____

**Remember to have your own relationship with God.**

**What's your favorite colors? (Colors has a special relationship to spiritual.)**

_____

_____

_____

_____

_____

_____

_____

_____

_____

_____

_____

_____

_____

_____

_____

_____

_____

_____

_____

_____

_____

_____

**Reading is power!**

**What do you appreciate most about family or least appreciated?**

_____

_____

_____

_____

_____

_____

_____

_____

_____

_____

_____

_____

_____

_____

_____

_____

_____

_____

_____

_____

_____

_____

_____

_____

_____

_____

_____

_____

_____

_____

_____

_____

_____

_____

_____

_____

_____

_____

_____

_____

_____

_____

_____

_____

_____

_____

**Always treat people with respect!**

**Mediating is the best self- care to give yourself: No phones, No Music Just You and God.**

_____
_____
_____
_____
_____
_____
_____
_____
_____
_____
_____
_____
_____
_____
_____
_____
_____
_____
_____
_____
_____
_____
_____

_____

_____

_____

_____

_____

_____

_____

_____

_____

_____

_____

_____

_____

_____

_____

_____

_____

_____

_____

_____

_____

_____

_____

_____

_____

_____

**Self- care is the Best Care!**

**Reading is the Key to Life: What's your favorite book & why?**

_____

_____

_____

_____

_____

_____

_____

_____

_____

_____

_____

_____

_____

_____

_____

_____

_____

_____

_____

_____

_____

_____

_____

_____

_____

_____

_____

_____

_____

_____

_____

_____

_____

_____

_____

_____

_____

_____

_____

_____

_____

_____

_____

_____

_____

_____

_____

_____

**Write your dreams down: they will manifest into reality!**

**Do you struggle with goals settings: first steps write them all down!**

---

**The World Depending on You!**

**Enjoy reading writing and thinking outdoors in nature: it gives you a totally different mindset.**

Sitting by the water is the best way to visit with God.

# Do you want to be notable or rich?

**God is still in control!**

**Pray without two faces: How much do you trust God with your life?**

_____

_____

_____

_____

_____

_____

_____

_____

_____

_____

_____

_____

_____

_____

_____

_____

_____

_____

_____

_____

_____

_____

_____

_____

_____
_____
_____
_____
_____
_____
_____
_____
_____
_____
_____
_____
_____
_____
_____
_____
_____
_____
_____
_____
_____
_____
_____
_____
_____
_____
_____
_____
_____

**Pray on your knees it's major respect to God!**

**Share your experience when you felt God presents for the first time?**

_____

_____

_____

_____

_____

_____

_____

_____

_____

_____

_____

_____

_____

_____

_____

_____

_____

_____

_____

_____

_____

_____

_____

_____

_____

_____

_____

_____

_____

_____

_____

_____

_____

_____

_____

_____

_____

_____

_____

_____

_____

_____

_____

_____

_____

_____

_____

_____

**God will always be with you every step of the way- allow Him to lead!**

# Stay prayed up never give up!

_____

_____

_____

_____

_____

_____

_____

_____

_____

_____

_____

_____

_____

_____

_____

_____

_____

_____

_____

_____

_____

_____

_____

_____

_____

_____

_____

_____

_____

_____

_____

_____

_____

_____

_____

_____

_____

_____

_____

_____

_____

_____

_____

_____

_____

**We Are Important to God He need us to survive.**

**Speak into your life: it will strengthen your growth in greatness. +**

_____
_____
_____
_____
_____
_____
_____
_____
_____
_____
_____
_____
_____
_____
_____
_____
_____
_____
_____
_____
_____
_____
_____
_____
_____

**When you love you more others can love you better!**

# Pray to your ancestors they're there to listen

_____

_____

_____

_____

_____

_____

_____

_____

_____

_____

_____

_____

_____

_____

_____

_____

_____

_____

_____

_____

_____

_____

_____

_____

_____

_____

_____

_____

_____

_____

_____

_____

_____

_____

_____

_____

_____

_____

_____

_____

_____

_____

_____

_____

_____

_____

_____

_____

_____

_____

**They paved our way, so they already know. Let Go and Let God!**

# God Don't Wont Beat Us He Want to Bless Us

_____

_____

_____

_____

_____

_____

_____

_____

_____

_____

_____

_____

_____

_____

_____

_____

_____

_____

_____

_____

_____

_____

**God bless you now and forever!**

# God Don't Want to Beat Us He Want to Bless Us

_____

_____

_____

_____

_____

_____

_____

_____

_____

_____

_____

_____

_____

_____

_____

_____

_____

_____

_____

_____

_____

_____

_____

_____

_____

**God we worship you for who you are!**

# God Don't Want Beat Us He Want to Bless Us!

_____

_____

_____

_____

_____

_____

_____

_____

_____

_____

_____

_____

_____

_____

_____

_____

_____

_____

_____

_____

_____

_____

_____

_____

_____

_____

_____

_____

_____

_____

_____

_____

_____

_____

_____

_____

_____

_____

_____

_____

_____

_____

_____

_____

_____

_____

_____

_____

**I can see you now risen!**

*Photo by Queen Vanessa*

WHEN I THINK OF MY LIFE, I THINK OF THE
WONDERFUL WORKS OF GOD HANDS.

*God Don't Want to Beat Us He Want to*
*Bless Us* has been developed and created
to help you understand, the ways of the
world have nothing to do with you.
Sometimes we beat ourselves up. That's a weapon
satan use against us it's called low-self-esteem.

satan will kill steal and destroy you and
all your works, our children, families
and communities. Don't let (it)
We must STOP, beating ourselves and loving
ourselves and trust God loves you more. Just as
much as He loves our ancestors and If you only
believe in His works. I am a living witness. I'm a born
and raised urban survivor! Hood that is-. I learned
early in life to stop trying to do it alone. And join
forces with who can move mountains, cease the
winds and commanding the ocean waves to roar!"
Can you do that?

Do you know anybody that can?
I do we call him Jesus. Trust in Him for He'll be
your personal Lord and Savior, And He'll guide you
in the time of troubles: we're living in unprecedent
times, don't get left behind, know God for yourself.

I love that he calls me Daughter & Friend….

We heard 2Pac mama in Poetic Justice:

"Time Not Forever".

Printed in the United States
by Baker & Taylor Publisher Services